FOREWORD

Bradford in East Manchester still exists as an electoral ward, yet its historical identity has waned and its landscape has changed dramatically in recent times. The major regeneration projects that created the Commonwealth Games sports complex and ancillary developments have transformed a former heavily industrialised area that had become run-down. Another transformation commenced much further back in time, though, when nearly 150 years ago this area changed from a predominantly rural backwater to an industrial and residential hub of the booming city of Manchester, which in the first half of the nineteenth century became the world's leading manufacturing centre. By the 1870s, over 15,000 people were living cheek-by-jowl with iconic symbols of the industrial age: a colliery; canals; cotton mills; and ironworks. These industrial structures were for the most part demolished in the late twentieth century, yet below-ground remains have often survived to a remarkable degree. It is the story of this archaeology, closely linked with over 600 years of historical and technological development, that is told here. These tangible remains allow us to reconnect with and appreciate Bradford's important industrial past.

Spreading the word about Manchester's fascinating but relatively unrecognised archaeology is challenging. One of the ways to do this is through publication in the form of 'popular' booklets. I have considerable pleasure therefore in introducing you to this publication, which is Volume 4 in a new series covering not only Manchester city's wonderful archaeology but also that of the whole of the Greater Manchester area: Bolton, Bury, Manchester, Oldham, Rochdale, Salford, Stockport, Tameside, Trafford and Wigan. This new series is called '*Greater Manchester's Past Revealed*', and provides a format for publishing significant archaeology from developer-funded, research or community projects in an attractive, easy to read, and well-illustrated style.

NORMAN REDHEAD, **County Archaeologist, Greater Manchester**

CONTENTS

Aerial view of Sportcity, looking north-eastwards towards the Medlock Valley (© webbaviation)

Today, the historic township of Bradford in East Manchester is dominated by the City of Manchester Stadium. Often referred to as Eastlands, this state-of-the-art arena forms the centrepiece for a suite of sporting venues developed to host the Commonwealth Games that were held in Manchester in 2002. These include the Regional Athletics Arena, Manchester Velodrome, the National Squash Centre, and the Manchester Tennis Centre, creating the largest concentration of world-class sporting facilities in Europe, known appropriately as Sportcity.

Previously, the area was a heavily industrialised district that was widely regarded as the 'engine room' for Manchester. Central to this reputation were the rich seams of coal that are known to have been mined in Bradford since the sixteenth century. However, it was not until the mid-nineteenth century that Bradford evolved rapidly from a sparsely populated rural township, centred on a moated manor house, to an important industrial area. An initial stage in this transformation was an expansion of Bradford Colliery to become the largest coal mine in the Manchester Coalfield, and the principal supplier of fuel to local steam-powered factories and domestic hearths. In the early 1850s, the famous Bradford Ironworks of Richard Johnson

Aerial view across Bradford in the 1950s
(Manchester Local Studies)

& Nephew was established adjacent to Bradford Colliery, and promptly developed an international reputation for revolutionising the wire-manufacturing industry. By the end of the nineteenth century, the colliery and the ironworks were surrounded by a range of textile mills, rubber works, chemical factories, brickworks, and a large gas works, interspersed with streets of terraced housing.

The demise of Manchester's manufacturing industries, including the closure of Bradford Colliery and Johnson & Nephew's works in the second half of the twentieth century, left tracts of disused brownfield sites and contributed to the economic decline of the area. The Commonwealth Games and the associated development of Sportcity brought a significant reversal of this trend, bringing new life to derelict industrial land, and providing a flagship for the wider renewal scheme for East Manchester.

The remediation and site-servicing works in progress during November 2010 (© www.SuaveAirPhotos.co.uk)

In order to ensure the economic value of the City of Manchester Stadium after the Commonwealth Games had finished, it was leased by the City Council to Manchester City Football Club (MCFC) for use as its home ground. In 2010, MCFC signed an agreement with the City Council to allow a £1 billion redevelopment of approximately seven hectares of brownfield land immediately to the east of the stadium, which included the sites of Bradford Colliery and Bradford Ironworks. As an initial stage, it was proposed that remediation and site-servicing works were carried out to treat soils contaminated by the site's former industrial use, and to decommission and remove associated buried structures.

These necessary works would clearly destroy any buried remains of the colliery, ironworks and other sites of archaeological interest, remains that could potentially yield important evidence for their historical development. Consequently, the Greater Manchester Archaeological Unit (GMAU), which provides advice to Manchester City Council, recommended that an archaeological investigation of the site was undertaken prior to the ground works. This was carried out by Oxford Archaeology North (OA North) in 2010 and, in the first instance, a series of trial trenches was excavated across the site. The trenches showed that some significant remains of Bradford Colliery, Bradford Ironworks, and two nineteenth-century textile mills survived *in-situ*, and merited further investigation.

Several larger areas were excavated subsequently across these sites. A trench was also placed across the position of the moat associated with the medieval Bradford Old Hall, elements of which had been excavated in 2002. This booklet presents the exciting findings from these archaeological excavations, and also summarises the development of the historic township of Bradford.

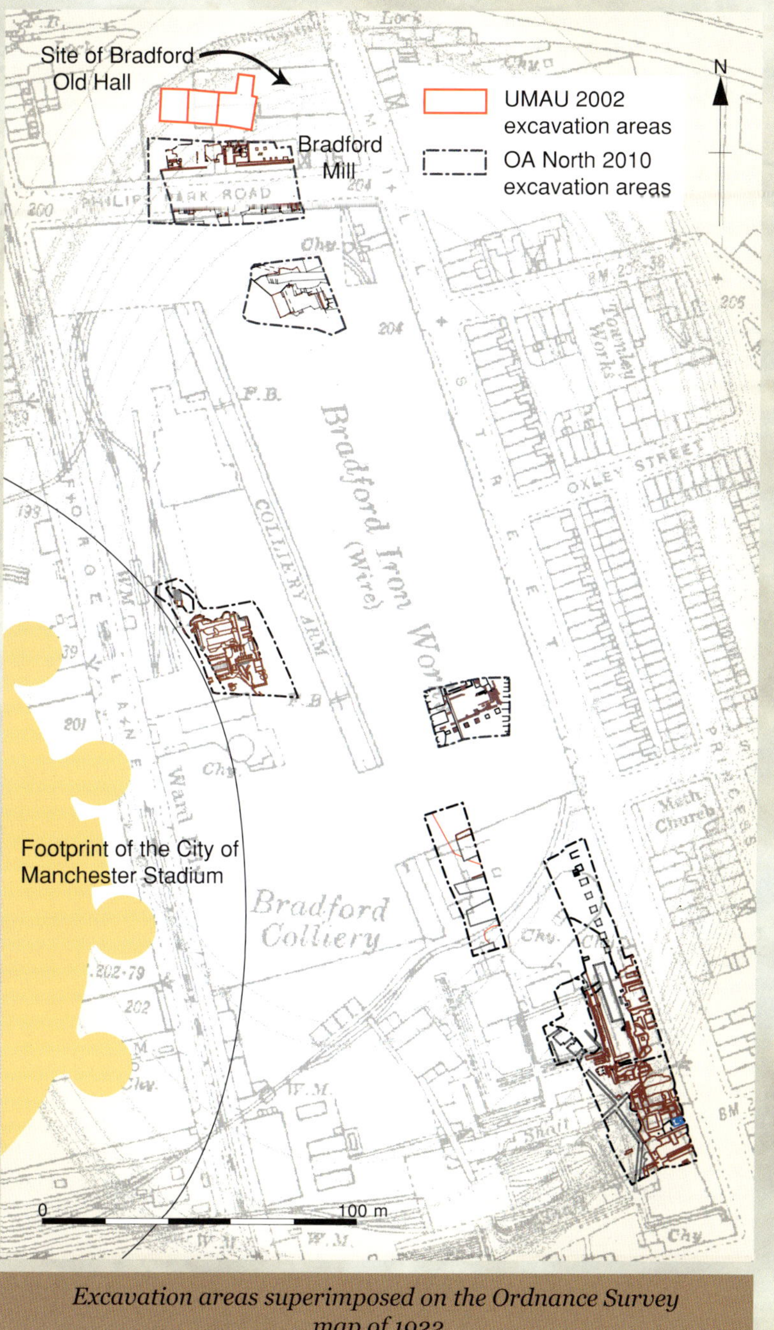

Excavation areas superimposed on the Ordnance Survey map of 1922

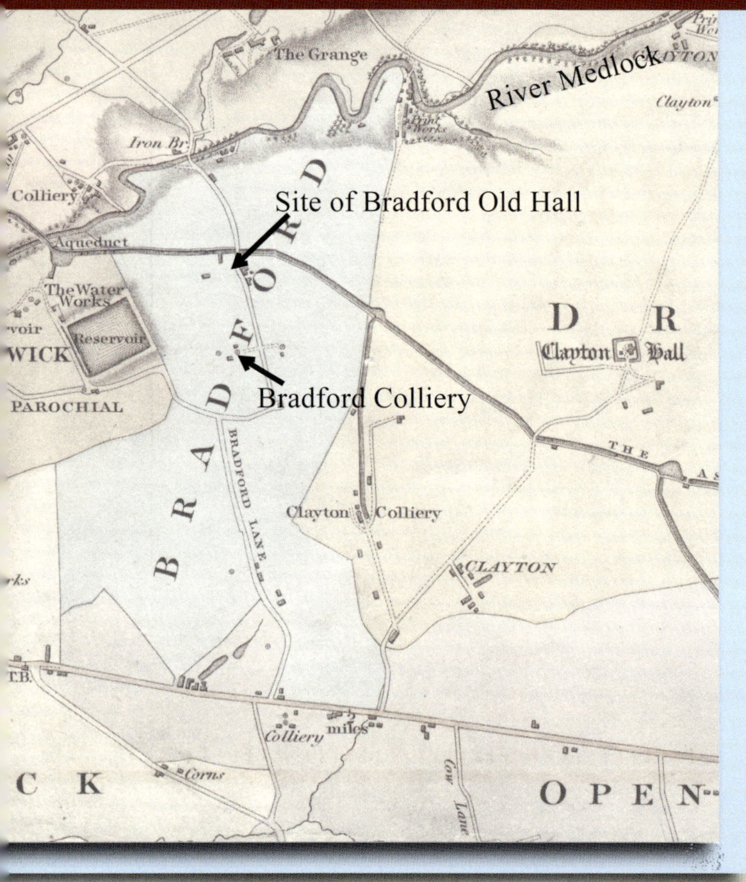

Extract from Johnson's Plan of the Parish of Manchester *of 1820*

The historic township of Bradford lies some 3km to the east of Manchester city centre, and covers approximately 116 hectares between the River Medlock in the north, Beswick and Openshaw to the south, and Clayton and Droylsden to the east. Notwithstanding alterations wrought by modern landscaping, the natural topography has a fairly level terrain, with slightly elevated ground in the area that was occupied in the medieval period by Bradford Old Hall. Further to the north, the ground level falls gently to the River Medlock. Until the mid-nineteenth century, this soft landscape supported a mixture of woodland and pasture, with water meadows alongside the river.

The River Medlock rises in the hills above Oldham, and flows westwards through Clayton and Bradford to join the River Irwell in the centre of Manchester. Whilst only a relatively small river, the Medlock has a history of bursting its banks, the most disastrous flood occurring in July 1872, when water swept through part of Bradford cemetery, washing coffins and corpses out of the ground and carrying them downstream. As a result of this disaster, sections of the river through Bradford were straightened, including a culverted stretch that flows beneath the northern end of Sportcity.

The Manchester Coalfield

Bradford lies on the Manchester Coalfield, which extends for some 6½km through East Manchester, and is up to 2½km wide. It is enclosed almost entirely by strata of red sandstone, which separates the Manchester Coalfield from the South-West Lancashire and Oldham coalfields. This rich natural resource was the basis of Bradford's economy for more than three centuries, and was the principal factor in the industrial development of the area. It has been estimated that more than 10,000 tons of coal per year was being used in Manchester by 1700, and a large proportion of this came from Bradford and the adjacent township of Droylsden. By 1940, more than 240,000 tons of coal per year were being mined from Bradford Colliery alone.

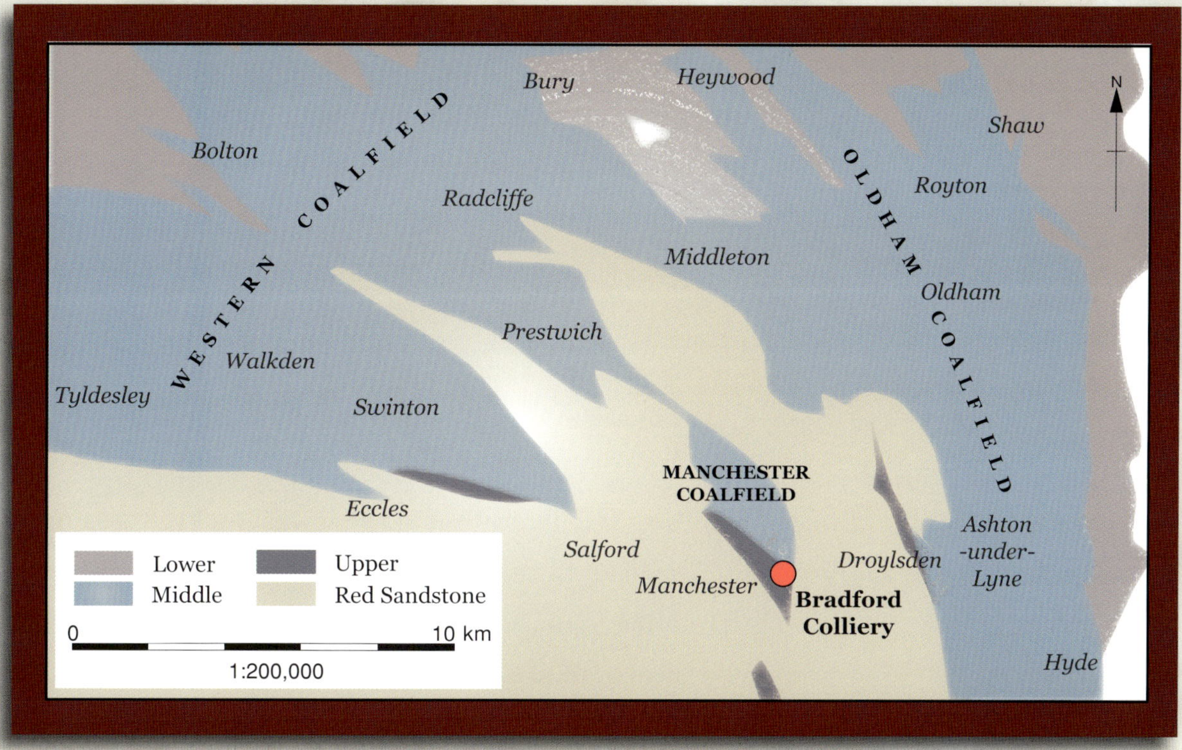

The South-East Lancashire Coalfield, showing the Upper, Middle, and Lower Coal Measures, and the extent of the Manchester Coalfield

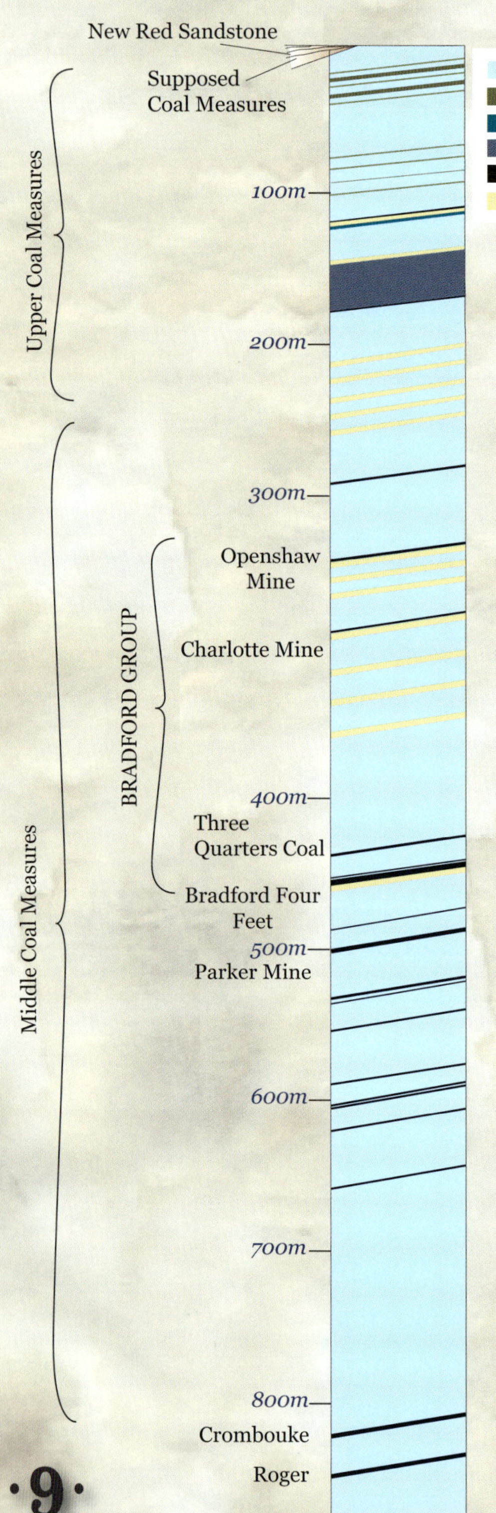

During the eighteenth century, the coal will have been gained from thin seams that could be found within a few metres of the surface. However, by the mid-nineteenth century, coal was being extracted via deep shafts from several different seams, which essentially yielded four types of coal, namely gas coal, household coal, manufacturing coal and steam coal.

The Upper Coal Measures form the highest commercially viable beds of the Manchester Coalfield, and comprise two thin seams of coal between bands of shale, limestone and sandstone. Below this, at a depth of approximately 250m beneath the surface, are the Middle Coal Measures. These contain a series of coal beds known collectively as the Bradford Group. Separated by bands of shale and fireclay, this group of productive coal seams includes the Openshaw Mine, Charlotte Mine, Three Quarters Coal, and the Bradford Four Feet. Situated at a depth of about 465m, the Bradford Four Feet is the lowest and thickest of these seams. Beneath the Bradford Group is the Parker Mine, lying at a depth in excess of 500m. The deepest coal beds are the Crombouke and Roger seams, which lie at more than 845m below the surface.

Schematic section through the Manchester Coalfield strata

THE MEDIEVAL HALL

The early history of Bradford is not well known. A third-century Roman coin, reported to have been discovered in Philips Park, represents the earliest evidence for human activity in the area. However, this was an isolated find, and whilst a Roman road between Manchester and York is thought to have taken a course a short distance to the north-west, there is no firm evidence for any Roman settlement in Bradford.

The name Bradford probably derived from Old English, and may be translated as 'wide ford'. This perhaps referred to an ancient crossing point over the River Medlock, although the earliest documented reference to Bradford dates to the 1160s.

By the late thirteenth century, Bradford formed part of the demesne land of the lords of Manchester. Settlement was probably focused on Bradford Old Hall, a manor house surrounded by a moat. There are an estimated 70 moated sites in Greater Manchester, with Ordsall Hall in Salford and Clayton Hall providing surviving examples of manor houses. The evidence derived from excavations of this

Early nineteenth-century engraving of Clayton Hall and its moat

type of site suggests that the heyday for their construction was between the late thirteenth and mid-fourteenth centuries.

The exact date at which Bradford Old Hall was erected is uncertain, although it is not mentioned in surveys of the Lord of Manchester's estate carried out in 1282 and 1322. It was possibly built between the 1330s and 1350s, when the manor of Bradford was held by John de Salford of Wakerley (Worsley). In 1357, the Lord of Manchester granted the manor to Thomas de Booth of Barton, and documents of that time refer to the Bradford estate as including a 'messuage', or dwelling. The Booths still owned Bradford Hall in 1513, when John Booth was killed at the Battle of Flodden in Northumberland, fighting a Scottish invasion led by King James IV. The final reference to the hall is in a rate book of 1717-18, and it seems to have been demolished shortly afterwards. The earliest plan of the site dates to 1761, and clearly shows the moat enclosing a square-shaped parcel of land, covered with trees. Access across the moat was probably via a wooden bridge on its south side.

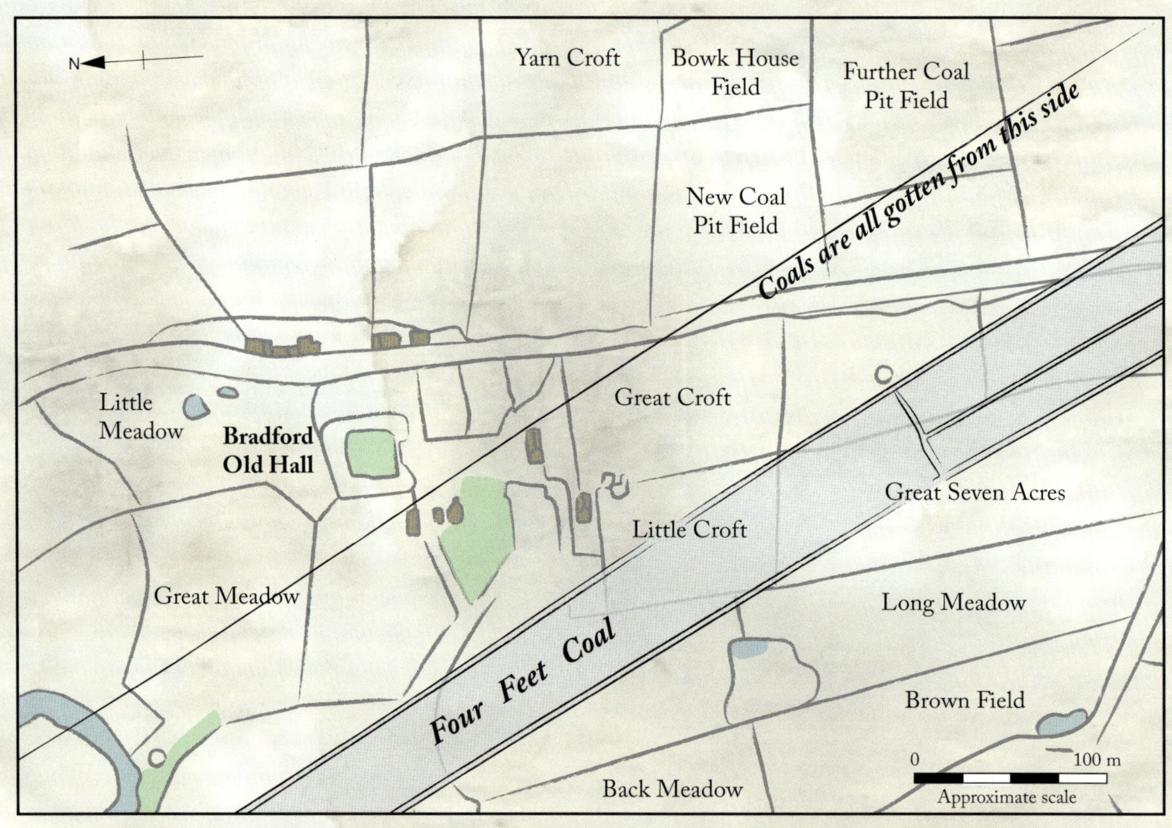

Copy of a plan of 1761, showing the medieval moat and the below-ground mine workings

In 2002, immediately prior to the construction of a Metro-link tunnel under Alan Turing Way, the University of Manchester Archaeological Unit (UMAU) carried out an excavation in the area of the moat. A thick deposit of silty clay containing organic material was exposed beneath the brick foundations of a nineteenth-century building, which lay on top of the eastern arm of the moat. This deposit was excavated to a depth of 3m with no discernible change in material, leading to a conclusion that this may have been the fill of the moat.

Excavation to the north exposed similar organic material, together with the remains of a wall that was composed of large, roughly hewn, red sandstone blocks. The largest of these measured 450 x 450 x 170mm, and had tool marks creating a decorative herringbone pattern. The wall was aligned north-north-west to south-south-east, and was interpreted as the inner face of the revetment wall for the eastern arm of the moat. Excavation further to the north revealed another section of wall, which comprised smaller fragments of limestone and yellow sandstone, compacted into a matrix of clay. It seemed possible that this represented a foundation of a wall for a building situated on the moated platform. Set between the stones were the stumps of two oak posts, together with several wooden stakes.

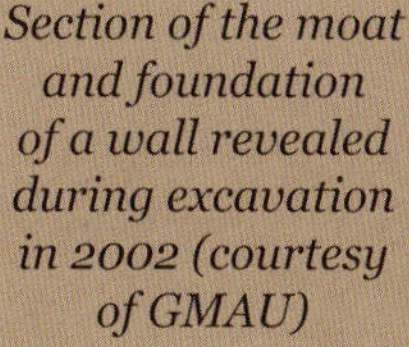

Section of the moat and foundation of a wall revealed during excavation in 2002 (courtesy of GMAU)

EARLY COAL MINING

It is known from historical documents that coal has been mined in Bradford since at least the late sixteenth century, and there are several burial records for men who were killed at 'Bradford Colepitte' in the seventeenth century. During this period, coal will have been extracted from thin seams that lay close to the surface. The workings may have been in the form of bell pits, with the miners working outwards from a central shaft that was rarely deeper than 10m. Typically, as no supports were used, only small amounts of coal could be gained before the pit became too dangerous to continue.

Cross-section of bell pits

In order to extract larger quantities of coal, and exploit the deeper seams, different mining methods were required. A common technique was 'pillar and stall', whereby shafts were sunk to depth and tunnels were then mined along the coal seam. These became the main haulage roads, from which were mined small roadways known as headings. Stalls were worked out from the headings, with pillars of coal left in place to support the roof of the workings.

A stylised nineteenth-century engraving showing miners hewing coal from stalls, leaving pillars for support

A variation of this method was the bank system of mining, where the excavated faces, or stalls, were much wider than the pillars. Another characteristic feature of the bank system was that it developed between two parallel haulage roads, which were extended as required to provide the necessary ventilation. Pillars of coal were left on either side of the bank for support, with the length of each bank being limited to a degree by haulage considerations. Waste material was packed into the space created from mining, known as the 'gob'.

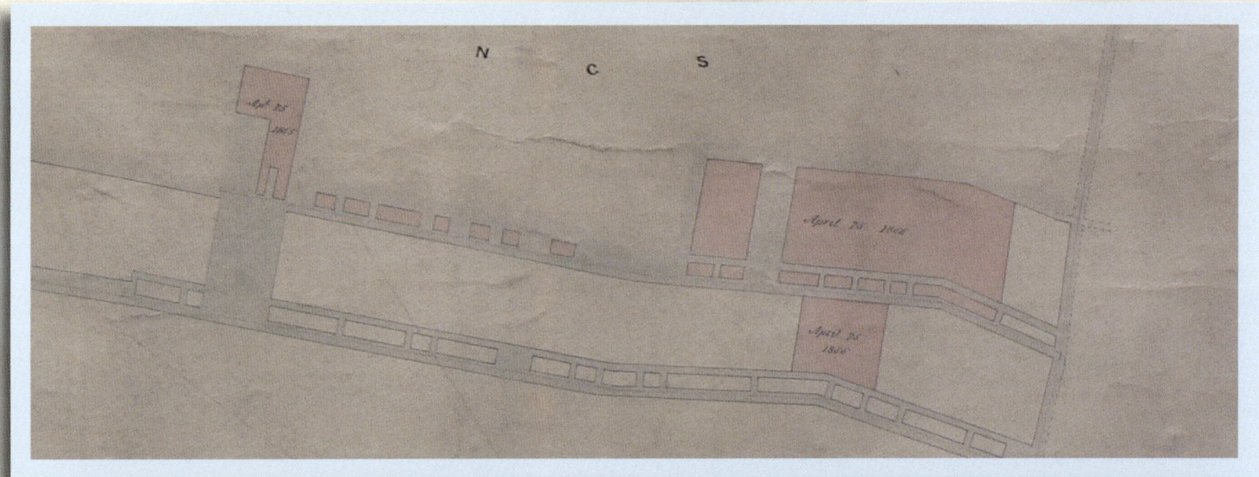

The characteristic layout of the bank system shown on a plan produced in 1854 of the workings in the Three Quarters Seam at Bradford Colliery

Field names are annotated upon the plan of Bradford of 1761, and these include 'New Coal Pit Field' and 'Further Coal Pit Field'. These probably refer to pit shafts, and reinforce the importance of coal mining to the local economy in the mid-eighteenth century. Other field names marked on the plan include 'Bowk House Field', 'Yarn Croft' and 'Great Croft', implying an area used for the open-air bleaching of cloth, and suggesting that some of the inhabitants of Bradford were engaged in producing textile goods.

The plan also marks the main underground workings of the Four Feet Seam, and shows a shaft at the site that became Bradford Colliery. However, this annotation was probably added at a later date, as the pumping and winding machinery required for deep-shaft mining had not been fully developed by the 1760s.

Numerous pit shafts, including two on the site of Bradford Old Hall, are also shown on an undated plan of Bradford that was probably drawn in the early nineteenth century. Again, a shaft is marked at the site that was to be developed as Bradford Colliery. The plan also depicts the underground workings to the north of the canal, the layout of which suggests that the mining methods employed were either 'pillar and stall' or the 'bank' system.

Early nineteenth-century plan of Bradford, showing numerous pit shafts and the underground workings

A view of a typical mid-nineteenth-century pit head, showing a steam-powered beam engine winding a trolley loaded with coal up the shaft, whilst an empty trolley is lowered down the adjacent shaft

The Lancashire coal-mining industry began to expand dramatically during the eighteenth century as the demand for coal increased. Between 1700 and 1830, it is estimated that the output from the Lancashire coalfields increased from 80,000 to 4,000,000 tons *per annum*. Such a growth in the industry required deeper shafts, which in turn demanded pumping machinery to drain the pits, and powerful engines for winding miners to the pit face and coal to the surface. These requirements were met successfully by the introduction of steam engines, which were used initially for pumping but, after the development of rotary motion in the 1780s, were also used for winding purposes.

Another crucial factor in the growth of coal mining was the emergence of an efficient transport network to deliver coal from the pit head to its market. In this respect, the opening of the Ashton-under-Lyne Canal in 1796 was a catalyst to the expansion of Bradford Colliery.

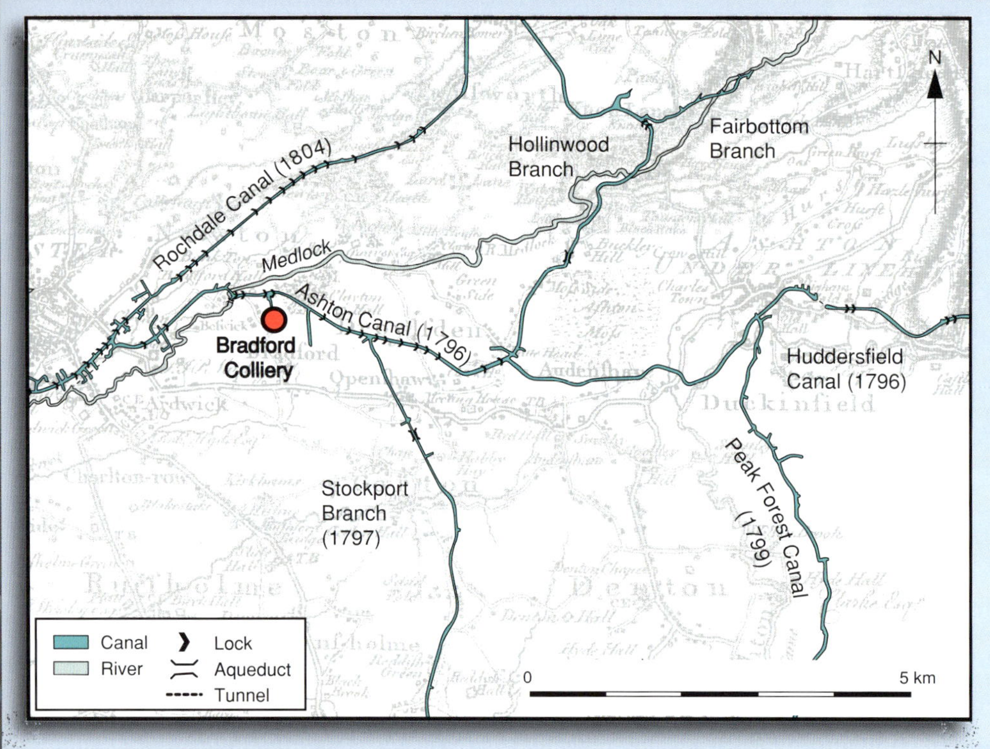

Route of the Ashton-under-Lyne Canal, superimposed on Yates' map of 1786

By 1792, England had been gripped by a 'canal mania'. This boom in canal-building followed the great success of the Worsley Canal, Britain's first true industrial canal, which provided the Duke of Bridgewater with a transport link between Manchester and his coal mines in Worsley. Eager to capitalise on the potential gains offered by this new form of bulk transport, a group of businessmen that included several colliery owners in Ashton-under-Lyne and Oldham put forward a proposal for an Act of Parliament to build a canal between Ashton-under-Lyne and Manchester, with branches to Stockport and Hollinwood, and a short spur to Dukinfield.

The original scheme was completed in 1796-7, although numerous branches that served factories and industry along its length were built subsequently. Amongst these branch canals was a short arm to Bradford Colliery, providing a direct route of communication between the pit head and central Manchester. Whilst it was not completed until the early 1840s, the northern end of this arm is

A view of the canal's route through Bradford in 1960, showing Stuart Street power station (Manchester Local Studies)

shown on the early nineteenth-century plan of Bradford, and appears to have utilised the western part of the abandoned moat around Bradford Old Hall. However, rather than having been designed for navigation, this may have been intended as a small reservoir for the short pound between the locks on either side of the junction.

The Bradford arm remained in use until the mid-twentieth century, as there are records of coal being transported by canal boat from Bradford Colliery during the Second World War. It is likely that the canal arm was also used as a drain for the colliery, receiving water pumped out of the deep shafts. This function may have ensured the retention of the canal for many years after canals had been superseded by railways and road freight as an efficient means of transporting coal. However, it went out of use with the closure of Bradford Colliery in 1968, and was infilled.

The buried remains of part of the canal were revealed by the archaeological works carried out in 2010. These remains included the eastern wall of the canal channel, which was exposed at a depth of 2.5m below the modern ground surface. This wall was 0.6m (2ft) thick, and was built using a combination of stone and brick.

The remains of the canal arm revealed in one of the initial evaluation trenches

The origins of Bradford Colliery are not documented, although by the early 1830s it was owned by T Porter Esq, whose injustice towards his miners was cited as the reason for industrial unrest that culminated in a strike during 1844. This may have led Porter to sell the colliery, as Messrs Clegg and Livesey, trading as the Bradford Colliery Company, had become the owners by 1845. The colliery was expanding at this time, and Bradford had begun to evolve from a rural area to an industrial settlement that was centred firmly on coal mining. This is reflected in the Census Returns for 1841, which show that a considerable proportion of the local male population was employed as miners at Bradford Colliery.

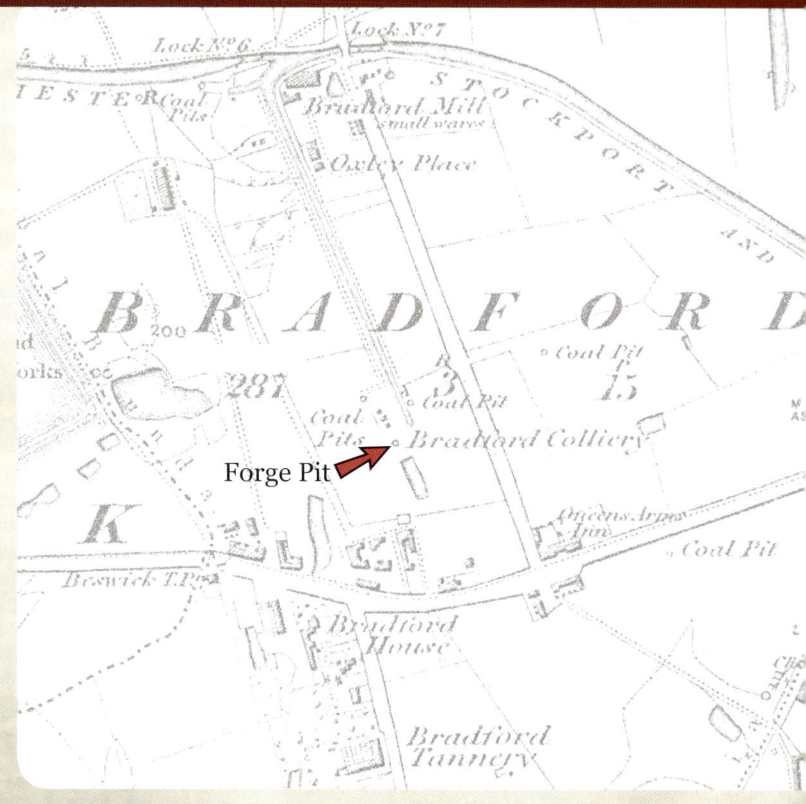

Extract from the Ordnance Survey map of 1848, which was surveyed in 184

The layout of the colliery in the mid-1840s is captured on Ordnance Survey mapping. This shows that the Bradford arm of the Ashton-under-Lyne Canal had been extended to the colliery. The map also depicts three shafts at the pit head, together with several small buildings. The southern shaft is likely to have been Forge Pit, one of the earliest deep shafts at the colliery, which was sunk to a depth in excess of 460m to reach the Bradford Four Feet Seam. Miners were lowered down the shaft by a rope attached to a manually powered capstan.

Forge Pit had an oval cross-section, and measured less than 3m across at its widest part. It was superseded in 1854, when Thomas Livesey opened the first of the modern shafts at the colliery, which had a diameter of 5.5m, and was sunk to a depth in excess of 500m to reach the Parker Seam. A second shaft, which became known as Little Pit, was sunk a short distance to the north-west and provided the ventilation required underground. Forge Pit was used thereafter for pumping water out of the workings.

Livesey's new shaft was equipped with a steam engine that was used for winding miners to the bottom of the pit, and also for hauling coal to the surface. This was installed in an engine house to the east of the shaft, whilst the steam required by the engine was raised in a bank of Lancashire boilers that was situated to the north.

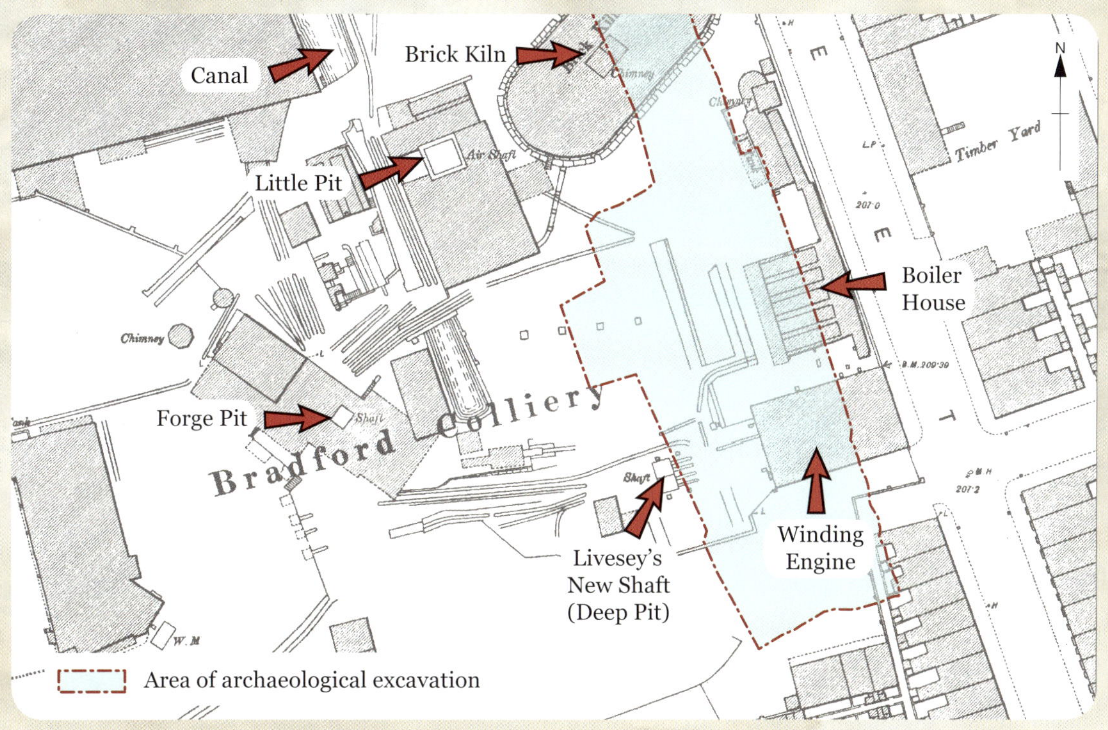

Extract from the Ordnance Survey map of 1891, showing the expansion of the colliery since 1845

The remains of the engine house exposed during excavation

The archaeological excavation revealed the buried remains of some of this infrastructure, including the substantial foundations of the engine house. This brick-built structure measured 20 x 12m, and incorporated a large pit that extended to a depth of nearly 4m below the floor of the building, and had probably housed the winding drum.

The front portion of the boiler house was also exposed during the excavation. This had originally contained five Lancashire boilers, although a sixth was added to the northern end at a slightly later date. A wide, brick-lined passage connected the boiler house with the top of the shaft, providing an easy route for carrying coal to the boilers.

The excavated remains of the nineteenth-century boiler house

Bradford Colliery Brickworks

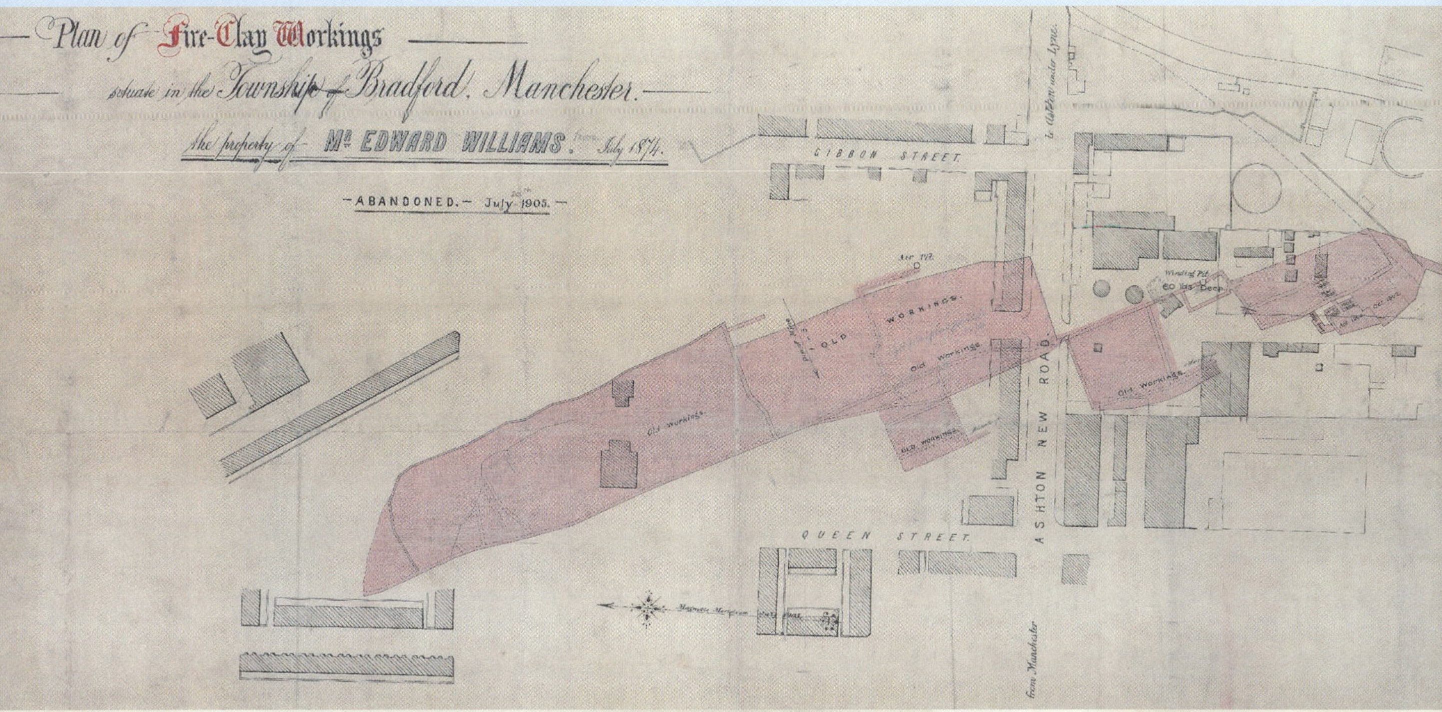

Plan of the underground fireclay workings at Bradford Colliery in 1874
(Plan NC acc 9529/M254, reproduced courtesy of the Archives Services Manager, Lancashire Archives)

In the early 1870s, the colliery manager, Edward Williams, decided to capitalise on the seams of fireclay that were found in the mine, and built a kiln for making tiles and bricks. These included refractory types that were required, amongst other uses, for lining the furnaces of an increasing number of ironworks in the area. Williams decided to build a large kiln, of an improved type, designed and patented by Friedrich Hoffmann in 1870.

This type of kiln could be kept working continuously, and was ideally suited for producing large quantities of bricks and tiles. They comprised a central barrel-arch, creating a circuit around the interior of the kiln, forming a passage for the fire. A series of chambers connected

The remains of a Hoffman-type brick kiln similar to the one that will have been at Bradford, revealed during an excavation at Oak Colliery in Oldham. This example was built in the 1880s

with the fire passage, and were separated from each other by a temporary 'wall' of combustible material. Pallets of fresh bricks were stacked in each chamber, ready for firing. Each chamber was fired for a specific time, and the fire was then guided to the adjacent chamber through careful control of the air flow. Fuel, frequently in the form of coal slack, was fed into the individual chambers from above, as required.

The brick kiln at Bradford Colliery was over 30m long and 17m wide, and probably contained either 12 or 14 firing chambers. It became one of the largest brick-making sites in the area, all their bricks bearing the trademark 'BC' stamp. However, despite the success of the brickworks, the fireclay workings were abandoned in 1903, and the kiln fell into disuse. It was eventually demolished in the late 1940s to allow for an expansion of the colliery.

The site of the kiln was a target for the archaeological excavation, although it was found to have been destroyed entirely during its demolition, leaving virtually no trace. This was perhaps surprising, given the substantial nature of the foundations for a kiln of this type.

Bradford Colliery in the Twentieth Century

In 1899, the Bradford Colliery Company was bought by the Fine Cotton Spinners' and Doublers' Association, an amalgamation of some of the largest cotton-spinning firms in Lancashire. The intention was to secure a cheap source of coal for their steam-powered mills in an attempt to reduce their costs in the face of increasing foreign competition. It was during this period that Livesey's shaft was extended to a depth of nearly 850m to reach the Crombouke Seam, as the Bradford Four Feet Seam had been exhausted. This became known as Deep Pit, and was reputed to be the second deepest mine shaft in the British coalfields. At this time, more than 500 miners were employed at the colliery.

*Installing a new headstock for Parker Pit in 1905
(Manchester Local Studies)*

The dawn of the twentieth century brought significant investment in the colliery. In 1900, an extensive electrical plant was installed, which was one of the earliest to be employed at a colliery. Three new electric motors supplied power underground to four haulage engines, two pumps and other machinery, whilst on the surface electricity was used to drive the screening plant and a carpenter's shop. However, steam power retained an important role and, in 1906, a new twin-cylinder steam engine was supplied by Robert Daglish of St Helens for winding at the Deep Pit. A second shaft was also sunk during this period. This was known as Parker Pit, and was intended as the ventilation, or upcast, shaft. However, it was also used for winding purposes, and was fitted with a twin-cylinder horizontal steam engine to power the winding gear.

View looking east across the colliery yard in c 1930, showing coal from the screening plant being loaded into various means of transport for distribution. The headgear for Deep Pit is clearly visible in front of the winding engine house, and the top of the headgear for Parker Pit can also be seen. The chimney on the far left is the derelict brick kiln.

Bradford Colliery was purchased in 1935 by Manchester Collieries Ltd, a large concern which, by 1940, owned 14 mines in the Lancashire Coalfield. In view of the favourable working conditions and the potential yield of high-quality coal at Bradford, the new owners implemented a major scheme of improvements in order to increase productivity. As an initial step, Deep Pit was extended into the Roger Seam, a rich deposit of high-grade coal that lay some 27m below the Crombouke Seam, and roadways, haulage and coal-face methods were also improved. As a result, the annual output increased from 171,557 tons in 1937 to 243,363 tons in 1940.

A new coal-preparation plant that was capable of handling 600 tons of coal per hour was also constructed, although this necessitated the demolition of the old brickworks, as there was no

An illustration by Fred Broadhurst showing miners being hauled to the coal face in the Crombouke Seam. Fred worked at Bradford Colliery as a Bevin Boy in 1946-8, and produced several unique drawings of the underground workings

land available to allow an expansion of the colliery's boundary on the surface. At this new plant, the coal was separated into different sizes by passing through primary screens, washed to extract the fines, and then screened again. The larger lumps of coal, usually ranging in size between 2" and 6", were either bagged automatically or loaded directly into lorries. Smaller coals were transferred to the land-sale yard, where it could be bought by local residents, saving the colliery company the expense of transportation costs.

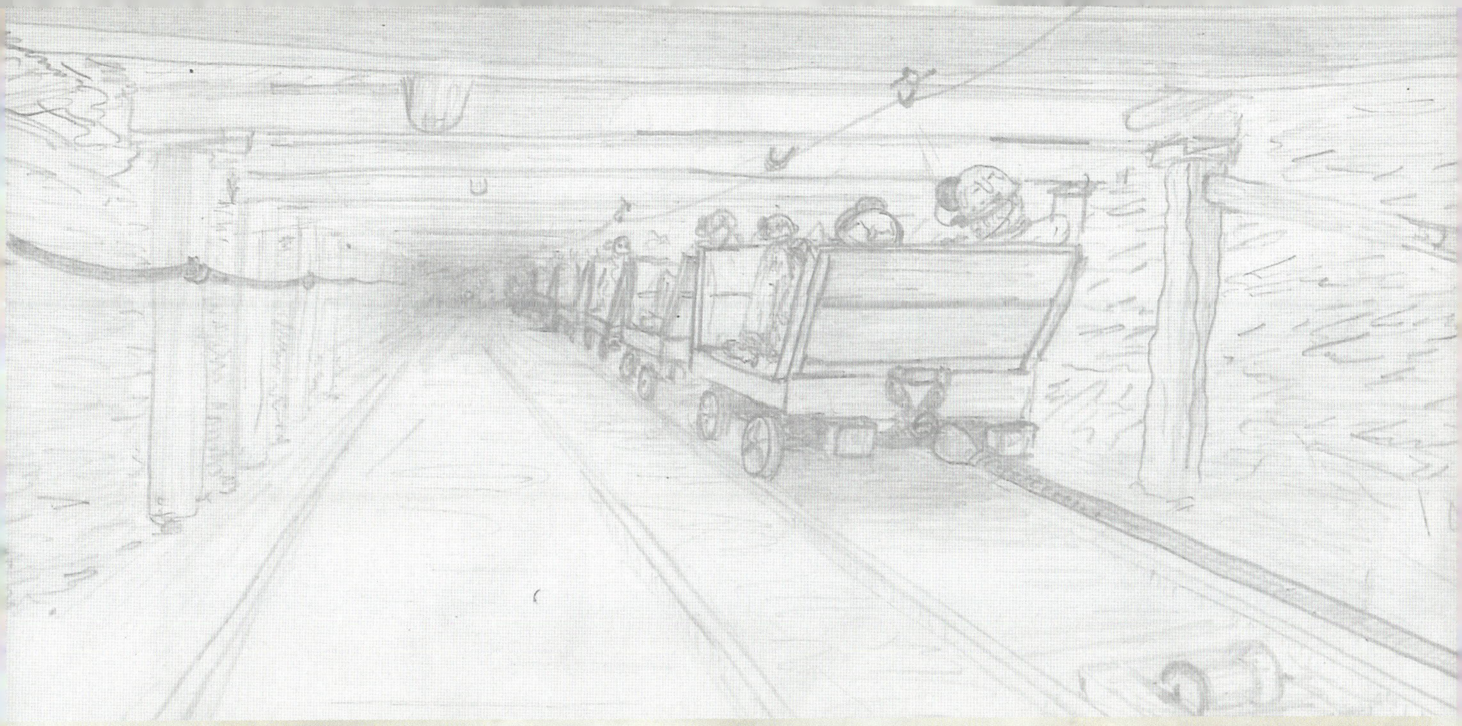

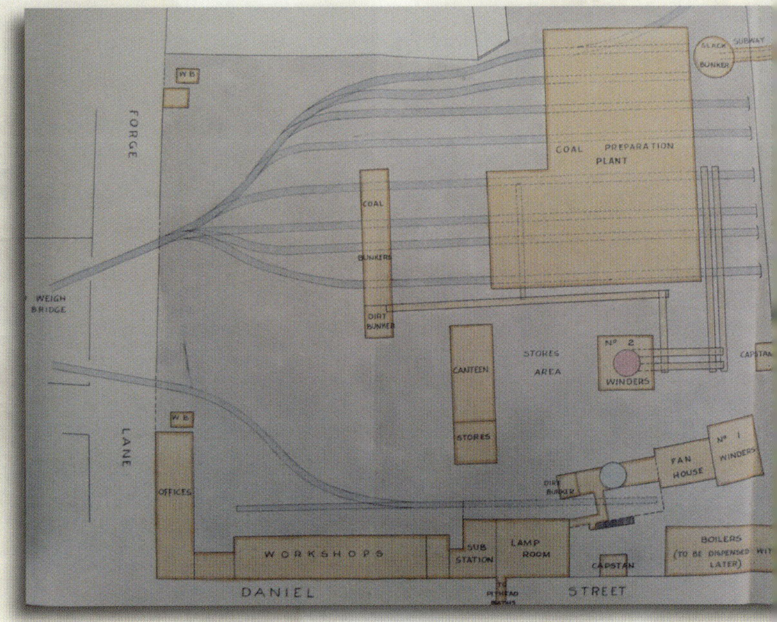

Design plan of 1945 for the new coal-preparation plant and tunnel to the Stuart Street power station

The smallest fragments of coal were mixed with the fines recovered from the washing process and sold to Manchester Corporation as fuel for their power station on Stuart Street. Coal was delivered directly to the power station via a conveyor belt, which was ingeniously laid in a 0.46km-long tunnel that passed beneath Mill Street and the Ashton-under-Lyne Canal.

Other improvements included the deepening of Parker Pit, which was sunk to the Roger Seam at a depth of 873m in 1948, and the installation of a new electric winder and headgear at Deep Pit. This was housed in a 200ft (60.96m) high reinforced-concrete tower, which was completed in 1953.

Stuart Street power station in 1973, with the derelict tower for the headgear at Deep Pit just visible
(Manchester Local Studies)

Excavating the remains of the coal-preparation plant

The buried remains of the coal-preparation plant dominated the northern part of the archaeological excavation area. These remains comprised numerous brick-built surfaces, reinforced-concrete foundations, and parts of the concrete baths that had been used for processing the coal.

In the 1960s, there were press reports that the colliery was causing serious subsidence in the area. Of particular concern was a gasholder on Bradford Road that had tilted so much that it could only be filled to half its capacity.

The final closure of the colliery was announced in 1968, although large reserves of the coal remained. At that date, nearly 1500 miners were employed, and daily output was averaging 2130 tons of saleable coal. The winding gear was demolished in 1973 and any other machinery that was not considered worth salvaging was buried on the site.

Demolition of the headgear in 1973
(Manchester Local Studies)

BRADFORD IRONWORKS

Portrait of Richard Johnson

Bradford Ironworks is famously associated with the celebrated firm of Richard Johnson & Nephew. The origins of this firm can be traced to 1773, when James Howard started in business as a pin-maker and wire-worker on Market Street Lane in Manchester. By 1817, Howard's business had passed into the ownership of John Johnson, and then to his two sons, Richard and William. By 1838, the firm was known as Richard Johnson & Brother, who had premises on Dale Street and Lees Street in the Ancoats area of east Manchester.

In 1853, Richard Johnson & Brother purchased land next to Bradford Colliery with the intention of building an ironworks. This housed puddling furnaces to convert pig iron produced in a blast furnace into wrought iron that could be used for manufacturing wire. These furnaces were designed to draw hot air over the iron without it coming into direct contact with the fuel, thereby keeping the impurities of the coal separated from the iron. The works also contained mechanical hammers and rolling mills that were required to process the iron ready for producing, or drawing-out, wire. This final stage in the manufacturing process was carried out at the firm's works on Lees Street.

Section through a puddling furnace

The manager of the new ironworks was George Bedson, who introduced several important technological advances that revolutionised the wire-making industry. In particular, in 1860 Bedson developed the first continuous galvanising plant, which coated the wire with zinc to protect it from rust. The success of this process led the firm to extend their works to the west in 1864, to establish a new galvanising plant. At the same time, the firm persuaded the Lancashire & Yorkshire Railway to build a new goods yard on adjacent land in return for guaranteeing a minimum traffic of 200 tons per week. It was during this period that William Johnson died, and Richard Johnson went into partnership with his nephew, creating the firm of Richard Johnson & Nephew.

Another key innovation developed by George Bedson was the continuous wire rod mill, which enabled 100lb (45kg) iron rods to be drawn in a single length of wire. The mill comprised a long series of rollers placed in pairs, alternately horizontally and vertically, with each incorporating a groove through which the iron rod passed. As it was drawn through each pair of rollers, the rod was reduced in section and extended proportionally in length.

In 1882, the firm ceased producing their own iron, and the wire-drawing processes were transferred from the old Lees Street works to Bradford. By that date, the firm was manufacturing up to 300 tons of telegraph cable every week, in addition to a diverse range of other iron and steel wire products. These included wire for upholsterers' springs and mattresses, brushes, spokes, chain welding wire, and barbed, solid and strand fencing wire.

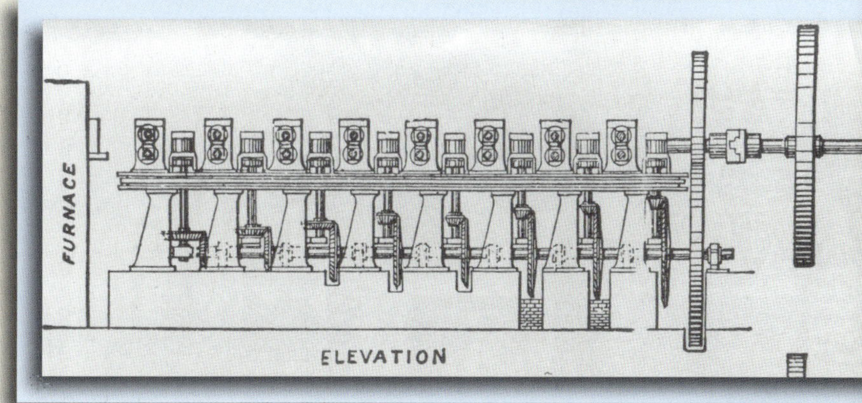

Section through Bedson's continuous wire rod mill, installed at Bradford Ironworks in 1862

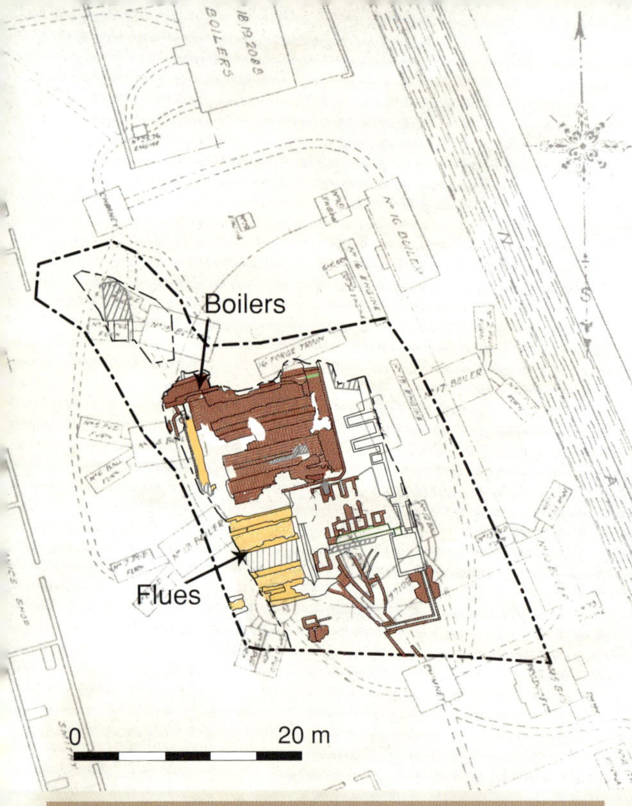

Plan of the excavated remains of Bradford Ironworks superimposed on a plan of 1873

The main working area of the original ironworks was targeted for archaeological excavation. A plan of the works dating to 1873 shows this part of the works as a semi-circular-shaped building that contained a series of boilers around the periphery, serving more than a dozen individual furnaces. These were linked to a network of flues, that led to a detached chimney on the southern side of the building. This plan also shows the steam-powered helve hammers and the forge train in the centre of the building.

However, the excavation demonstrated that this arrangement was remodelled during the late nineteenth century. The individual boilers were superseded by a bank of three larger boilers, and

Excavated remains of the late nineteenth-century boilers

Recording the remains of a flue for a regenerative furnace in Bradford Ironworks

a regenerative furnace was installed. The surviving remains of this furnace included several arched flues, each containing carefully laid stacks of firebricks, a characteristic feature of regenerative technology.

In 1904, the firm diversified into the production of copper and bronze wires, which became an important branch of their business. The outbreak of the First World War led to a rise in the demand for wire, and particularly barbed wire. In order to meet this demand, a new rod mill was built at the Bradford works, occupying land between the canal arm and Mill Street.

Inside the wire rod mill in c 1950

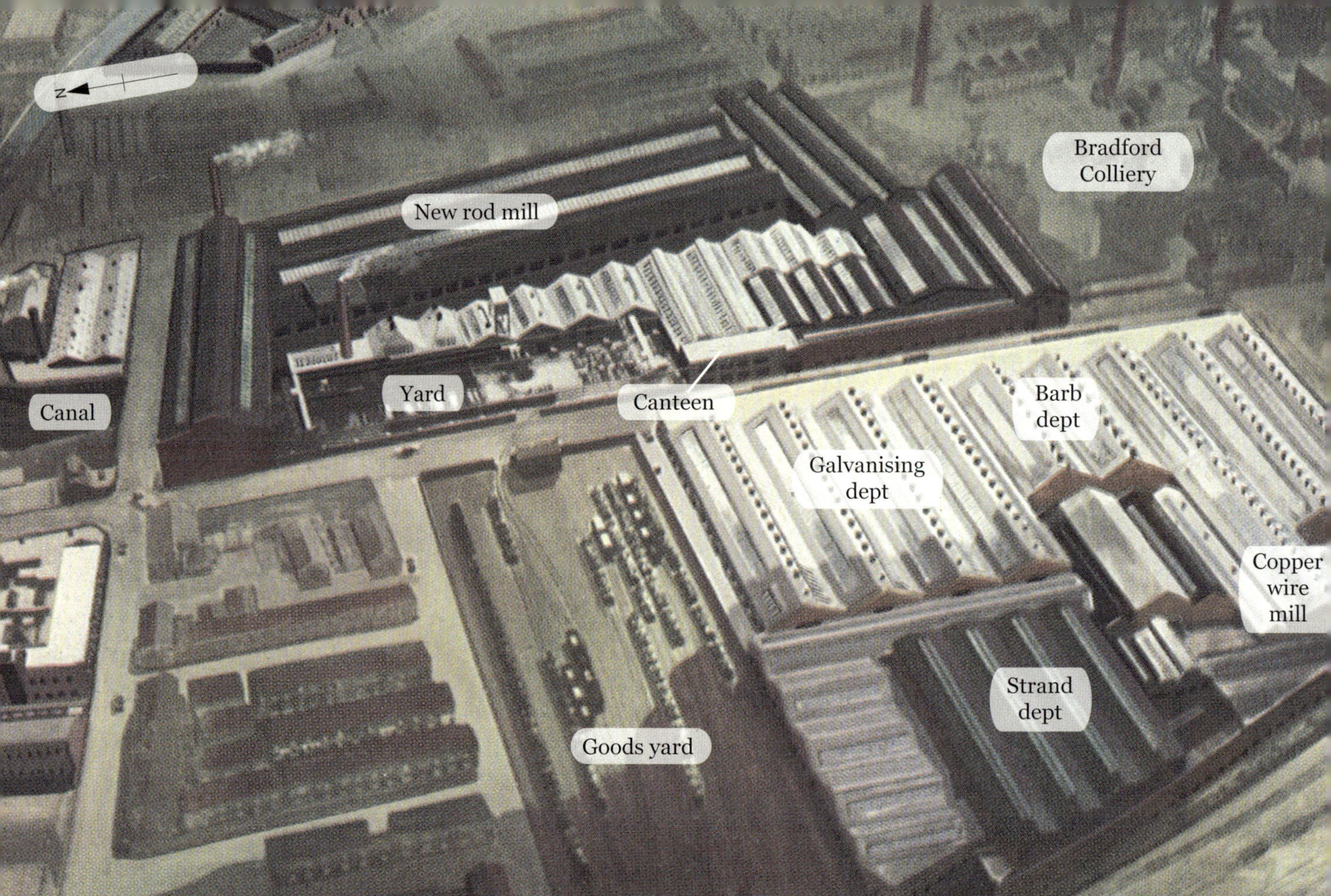

The extent and layout of the Bradford Works in the 1950s

During the initial trial trenching, the collapsed remains of several underground flues were excavated on the site of the twentieth-century wire rod mill. These were all constructed of firebricks, designed to withstand the very high temperatures associated with a furnace.

Further excavation of this area was carried out in an attempt to ascertain the nature and extent of these flues. This demonstrated that they had formed part of another regenerative furnace, although the very unstable condition of the remains meant that the archaeologists could not enter the excavated trench to study the structures in detail.

The adaptation of regenerative technology to an iron furnace was introduced by William Siemens in 1861, although several improvements and modifications were patented subsequently. This original furnace design contained two pairs of regenerative chambers beneath the furnace, each packed with bricks in a chequer-pattern of unbonded brick, stacked in such a way that gases could pass through. Hot exhaust gases leaving the furnace flowed downwards through one pair of regenerative chambers, imparting a substantial part of their heat to the brick chequerwork, on their way to the chimney. Once the bricks were sufficiently hot, the direction of gas flow in the system was reversed by a series of valves to allow the hot bricks to heat up the gas and air entering the furnace via the other pair of chambers, whilst the exhaust gases reheated the opposing pair. This pre-heating of gases produced a considerable reduction in fuel. William Siemens suggested the figure was as high as 70-80%.

A second breakthrough in the Siemens redesigning of the furnace was the removal of the coal-powered fireplace, and its replacement with a gas supply, located away from the furnace. The absence of any thick deposits of soot in the flues excavated at the site of the rod mill indicate that these furnaces had been gas fired.

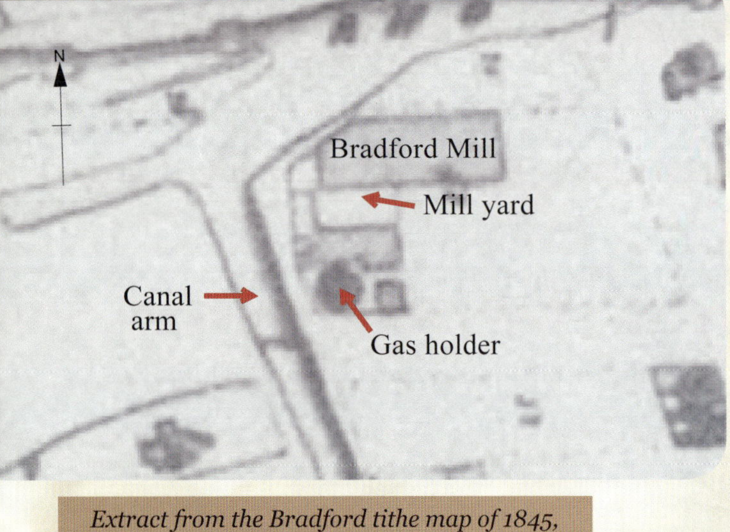

Extract from the Bradford tithe map of 1845, showing Bradford Mill

As Manchester emerged as the country's premier centre for the steam-powered cotton industry, textile factories became a feature of the surrounding townships, and Bradford was no exception. The earliest textile mill in Bradford was built on the site of the medieval hall in the 1840s. Known as Bradford Mill, it was owned by William Pritchard & Brothers, who produced a range of cotton goods classed as smallwares.

The mill appears on the Bradford tithe map of 1845, which shows a large building that was probably the main processing block, together with a smaller range to the south of a central yard. The map also depicts a large circular structure, almost certainly representing a gas holder that will have stored the gas used for lighting in the mill. Following the first successful installation of a gas-lighting system in a cotton mill by Samuel Clegg in 1805, this new technology was adopted by many mill owners. However, in the absence of a public supply, they each had to produce their own gas by baking coal in specially designed ovens, or retorts, and collecting the vapours that were released.

In 1864, the municipal gas works on Bradford Road was opened, and the huge gas holders that still dominate the local townscape were constructed, rendering the small gas plant at Bradford Mill superfluous to requirements. This was demolished in the 1860s to allow a new block to be added to the mill complex, which lay along the northern side of the newly constructed Philips Park Road.

Excavated remains of Bradford Mill, with Philips Park Road to the left

The footprint of the original mill lay beyond the area available for archaeological excavation in 2010. However, the foundations of the block erected in the 1860s were exposed, together with a buried section of Philips Park Road. This was more than 8m wide, and was composed of squared granite setts, creating a new main route heading west from Bradford to Ancoats through Beswick.

Excavation within the central part of the mill block revealed the remains of a loading bay, complete with a weighbridge. The area to the east had clearly been one of the processing areas in the mill, and contained a series of surfaces. The earliest of these comprised flagstones, into which a series of stone bases for machinery had been set. The flagstones had been overlain by a crude surface of bricks, marking a change in the use of the building. This may have been laid in the early twentieth century, when the mill was taken over by William Waite, Sons & Atkinson Ltd, a firm of hemp spinners, which used the building as a warehouse for their factory on Stuart Street.

Crude surface in the mill of bricks made at the Bradford Colliery

During the second half of the nineteenth century, several new textile factories were built in Bradford, serving different branches of the industry. These included flax and hemp spinning at Philips Park Mills, cotton spinning at Robert Marsland's Bradford Mill on nearby Gibbon Street, and the weaving of various cotton goods at Reservoir Mills, African Mills, and Sheldrake Mill, which all occupied sites alongside the Ashton-under-Lyne Canal. Another factory in the latter group was Park Mills, a large weaving factory that was established in the mid-1850s by Sharp, Murray & Co, who manufactured a type of cotton cloth known as gingham. Distinguished by its blue and white or green and white chequered pattern, gingham was one of the specialities of the Manchester mills.

Gingham cloth

Park Mills was built on undeveloped land between Mill Street and the Bradford canal arm, which was used as a supply of water for the mill's steam-power plant. Several streets of terraced housing, including Benson Street, were also built during this period to house the increasing number of workers required by the new factories.

Park Mills closed in the 1890s and, following demolition, two new streets of terraced housing were built on the site, although these were to be short-lived. Clearance of older dwellings on Benson Street to the north started in the early 1900s, and the newer houses were demolished shortly afterwards, to allow for an expansion of the Bradford Ironworks during the First World War.

*Derelict houses on Benson Street in 1904, awaiting demolition
(Manchester Local Studies)*

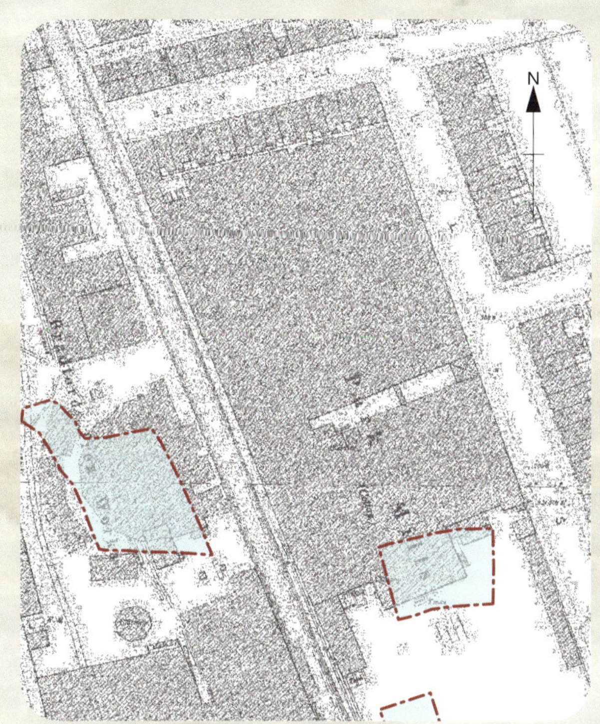

Excavation areas superimposed on the Ordnance Survey map of 1890

Even though the site had been redeveloped several times, some buried remains of the mill were revealed in the initial trial trenches. Further excavation was focused on a small rectangular block against the southern end of the main building, and was intended to ascertain whether this housed the steam engine and boilers, as a chimney is marked in this area on the Ordnance Survey map of 1890. Steam engines were frequently placed within the main processing blocks in early textile mills but, after the mid-nineteenth century, were increasingly housed in separate buildings.

The surviving remains exposed by excavation included the brick-built foundations and fragments of internal flooring. However, there was nothing to indicate that a steam engine had occupied this building, suggesting that the power plant had been sited within the main body of the mill.

The excavated remains of Park Mills, showing stanchion bases that formed part of the later ironworks

Bradford was an isolated rural township with few inhabitants throughout the medieval period. Notwithstanding the growth in coal-mining activity in subsequent centuries, there were still only 11 ratepayers recorded in Bradford in 1655. The local population had grown slightly by the end of the eighteenth century, although the Census for 1801 lists a mere 99 people living in the township, occupying a total of 94 houses. Most of the residents gave their occupation as miners.

The pace of growth accelerated during the next few decades and, between 1831 and 1851, the number of residents rose from 181 to 1572, and had more than doubled by 1861, to a total of 3523. Inevitably, this rise in the population was accompanied with a suite of social problems. In 1856, for instance, a petition was presented to the General Board of Health, requesting that the Public Health Act of 1848 was applied to the township of Bradford. Amongst the complaints cited by the petitioners was the prevalence of typhus in Bradford, whilst the air was said to be polluted with 'dense clouds of smoke from mill chimneys and iron forges... mingled with the smells from odorous manufactories, ashpits and filthy ditches'. An article printed in the *Ashton Reporter* in 1859 went as far as asking 'what can be worse than the aspect of Bradford and Beswick?'

The 1870s brought a rapid influx of families from central Manchester seeking work at the colliery and adjacent factories. By 1879, the local population had soared to an estimated 15,500. This was accompanied by the formation of local gangs, which became notorious for violent street fights known as 'scuttling'. An escalation in scuttling in Bradford was noted as a particular social problem in 1877, when local youths fought with gangs from the adjacent townships of Gorton and Openshaw. During one incident, in September 1877, the Bradford Scuttlers had a showdown with a gang from Pollard Street in Ancoats, a melée that involved no less than 500 youths, armed with knives, belts, sticks, pokers and bricks. By 1879, scuttling had escalated to such an extent that 'neither life nor property was safe'. Despite this rather damning sketch though, Bradford boasted Philips Park.

Philips Park

Philips Park was one of the first municipal parks in the world, and was a civic triumph of which Bradford was justifiably very proud. The need for public parks had been recognised by 1833, when the Parliamentary Select Committee on Public Walks reported as a matter of grave concern that the working-class residents of Manchester 'had no public walk or open space to take air and exercise in on Sundays, or after the arduous labours of the day'.

Philips Park was established by funds raised from public subscription, allowing the land to be purchased from the estate of Lady Hoghton for £6200. It was officially opened in August 1846

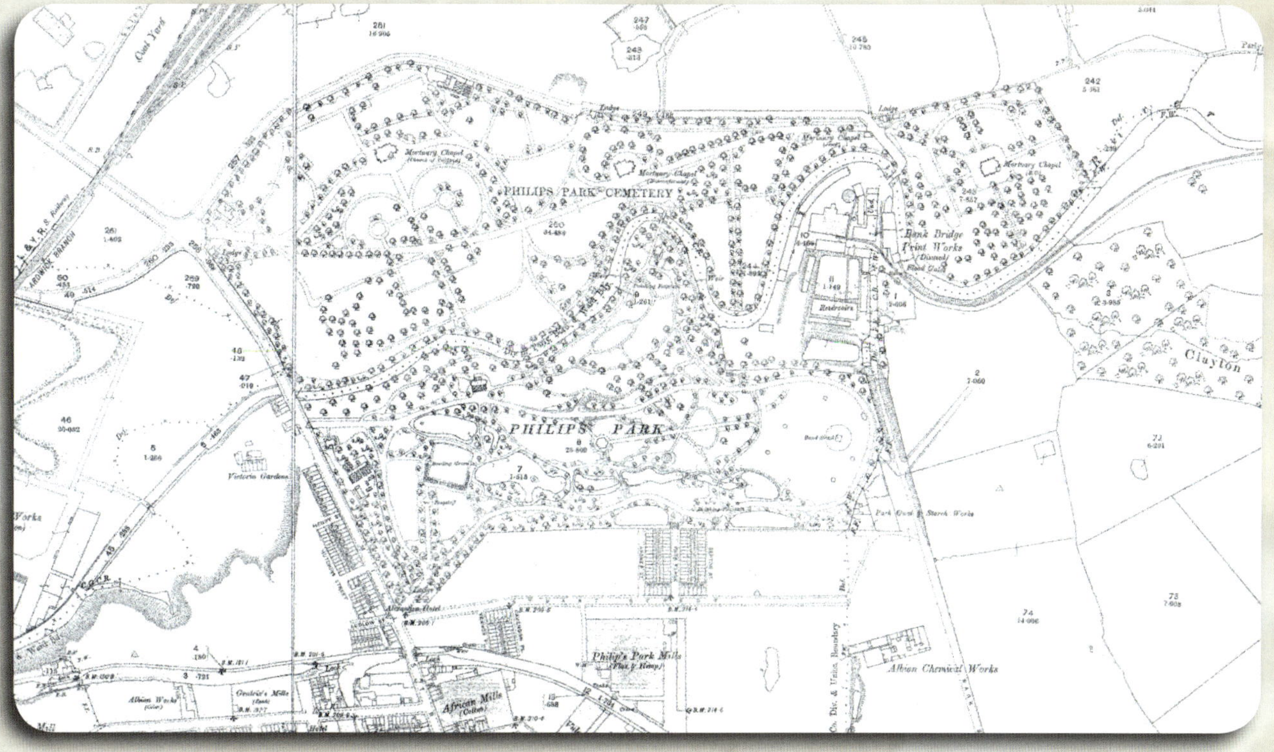

Philips Park, as shown on the Ordnance Survey map of 1893

A postcard view of Philips Park in 1930

and, together with Peel Park in Salford and Queen's Park in Harpurhey, was one of three public parks that were opened on the same day. The 12-hectare park took its name from a local MP, Mark Philips, who had campaigned intensively over many years for the creation of parks that could be used freely by Manchester's working population.

At its opening, the park was described in the *Manchester Guardian* as 'one of Manchester's greatest achievements'. Containing numerous ornamental flower beds with spectacular floral displays, it provided opportunities for recreation activities that included skittles, quoits, archery, cricket, and badminton, together with sports pitches and several children's play areas, which were connected via winding pathways interspersed with water features. In 1871, the park became one of the first in Manchester to boast a bowling green, and 20 years later one of the park's ponds was converted for use as the city's first open-air swimming pool. The park was a source of great civic pride, and was a hugely popular place for spending leisure hours, attracting as many as 30,000 visitors on a summer's day.

Amidst the bustle of the modern city, Philips Park continues to provide a haven for local residents and wildlife, and is still used for a wide range of leisure and sporting activities. In 2001, the park was added to the National Register of Parks and Gardens of Special Historic Interest in England, and is designated as a Grade II listed site to reflect its historical importance. More recently, the park was awarded Green Flag status, in recognition of it being one of the best green spaces in the country.

A view of Philips Park in 2010

The remediation works nearing completion in March 2011, showing the capping of the pit shaft in place (©SuaveAirPhotos.co.uk)

The archaeological excavations in Bradford were undertaken prior to the remediation and site-servicing works that were carried out to prepare the site for a major development, which will create leisure and employment opportunities for the local community, and contribute to the continued economic growth within Manchester. This project forms an important element of the wider scheme of renewal of East Manchester, which focuses on some 2000 hectares immediately east of the city centre, and is one of the largest programmes of urban regeneration carried out in Britain.

View across the remains of Bradford Colliery, revealed during the archaeological excavation

The archaeological investigation was undertaken by OA North to satisfy planning conditions for the remediation works. Manchester City Council attached these conditions to planning consent on the recommendation of GMAU, which also devised a specification for the scope of works required, and provided advice throughout the entire process, from starting the initial evaluation trenching through to publication of the results.

The programme of archaeological works was intended to establish whether any important buried remains survived within the site, and to make a detailed and accurate record of any that were found to exist. This process is known as 'preservation by record' and it leads to the creation of a technical report and site archive, which in this instance has been deposited with the Museum of Science and Industry in Manchester, where it can be consulted. This approach is in accordance with current national planning policies, which are set out in Planning Policy Statement PPS 5 *Planning for the Historic Environment.*

PPS 5 also stresses the importance of making the information generated from archaeological investigations publicly available. The intention of this booklet has been to achieve this aspiration, helping to rediscover Bradford as an important historic area, and charting its evolution from a rural idyll to the engine room of Manchester.

GLOSSARY

✴ BELL PIT: An early method of mining that involved the excavation of a vertical shaft to a depth not exceeding 10m, whereupon miners would work outwards along the seam until the risk of collapse became so great that the workings had to be abandoned. The name ascribed to the workings derived from their shape, which resembled a bell.

✴ BEVIN BOY: Young men conscripted to work in coal mines, from December 1943 until 1948.

✴ CAPSTAN: A revolving barrel with a vertical axis used for winding cables or ropes.

✴ MESSUAGE: A dwelling house and its surrounding buildings and lands used by the household.

✴ REGENERATIVE FURNACE: A type of furnace that operates at high temperatures by using preheated fuel and air for combustion. The hot exhaust gases from the furnace are pumped into a brick-filled chamber, where heat is transferred from the gases to the bricks. The flow of the furnace is then reversed so that fuel and air passes through the chamber and are heated by the bricks.

✴ TOWNSHIP: In England, a township was a sub-division of a large parish. This usage became largely obsolete during the late nineteenth century when local government reform converted many townships into civil parishes, formally separating the connection between the ecclesiastical functions of ancient parishes and the civil administrative functions.

FURTHER READING

- Bairsto, H, 1991 *Just Henry: Memories of Bradford and Moston Collieries*, Radcliffe

- Davies, A, 2008 *Gangs of Manchester*, Preston

- Hatcher, J, 1993 *The History of the British Coal Industry*, Oxford

- Hayes, G, 2004 *Collieries and their Railways in the Manchester Coalfields*, Ashbourne

- Johnson and Nephew Ltd, 1947 *The Part We Play*, Manchester

- Keaveney, E, and Brown, D L, 1974 *The Ashton Canal*, Manchester

- Seth-Smith, M, 1973 *Two Hundred Years of Richard Johnson & Nephew*, Manchester

- Walker, J S F, and Tindall, A S (eds), 1985 *Country Houses of Greater Manchester*, The Archaeology of Greater Manchester, **2**, Manchester

- Warrender, K, 2007 *Underground Manchester: Secrets of the City Revealed*, Altrincham

- Wyborn, T, 1995 *Parks for the People: The Development of Public Parks in Victorian Manchester*, Manchester Region History Review, **9**, 3-14

Further information on the history and development of Bradford is available at the Sportcity Visitors' Centre, which features a free exhibition of archive photographs, artefacts, and memorabilia from the area.
The Centre also has several original sketches by Fred Broadhurst of the underground workings at Bradford Colliery on display.

All of the historical maps reproduced in this booklet can be found at Manchester Local Studies within Manchester Central Library.

Historical images can also be viewed at http://images.manchester.gov.uk

A copy of the detailed excavation report, together with the project archive, has been deposited with the Museum of Science and Industry in Manchester.

Publications in The Greater Manchester Archaeological Journal, Greater Manchester Past Revealed *series,* The Archaeology of Greater Manchester *series, and* The Heritage Atlas *series are available from GMAU.*